The Cloudy Sky

Four Series of Verses

Traumear

Paperback ISBN 978-1-7948-7434-3

*

www.traumear.com

Four series of verses:

*

The Cloudy Sky

1

Every vestige of human life
Is compromised by how we behave.
We take this to our grave.
I am glad to put my cards on the table,
Order another round for the boys
(I myself am teetotal)
And I sit here quietly thinking.

Illusions are my best friends.
Nothing introduces itself to me
But I gently take it by the scruff
And persuade it to reveal its name to me.
In case of no name, I supply one.
I am a human being and I get annoyed
When the colander overflows.

A tricksy clown attends at my table.
What have you in mind, my friend?
Is it a complaint you have
A propos the tightness of your jeans?
Or perhaps you can no longer breathe?
I suggest you go out and mow the lawn
And then take a pensioner for a walk.

*

2

You are quite right,
There are too many beasts of burden
And not enough bearers of the light;
Congestion of the arteries is the consequence.

No shortage of villains and highwaymen,
That's true, and excuse me, before you get
On your high horse, would you condemn
The odd aspirin during a head-cold?

*

3

When I was young and impressionable
All things around me fell into place
And the bright light shining within me
Illuminated the world, both day and night.

Now I question every flower, every insect:
Do you know how lucky you are to be alive?
It hurts me to see so many lives wasted
By blind inconsequence in the light of day.

*

4

Derivative, these morning contemplations
Of an intriguing way forward that allows
Every possible permutation of grief and
Glory to settle into the nervous disposition.

I am no longer slavishly attached to your
Outer shell while the inner kernel rots.
Surely it depends on me what I make of
Rosy morning skies, a gulls harsh chatter.

*

5

Even if there were no fatigue, no outstanding
Lusts to be settled, I hope you know what I mean,
I would nonetheless cringe if anyone were to
Ask me to lambaste this horrible mood I'm in.

You see, I did not ask for it, it arrived on my
Doorstep and pleaded with me to allow it to
Hang a few scoundrels on local lamp posts for
Interfering repeatedly with the creative process.

*

6

This morning, like any other morning,
And yet, I would not exchange it for another.
The same old business of getting the juices
Flowing through the arteries and veins after
A night of tossing and turning under the coverlet.
Shōnagon, we share good memories, you and I.

What is literature? What was it, when it still
Held us enthralled in our innocence while we
Dreamt ourselves into forgetfulness of our duties?
Rain is dripping from the eaves this morning
And gurgling down the drain pipe. I can make
No promises of what might be achievable today.

*

7

Where would you be if you
Handled your affairs like a billionaire,
With one foot in the grave and the other
On a pile of gold? Does that sound attractive?
On the other hand, somebody has to do it.
It's bad character to want more.

More what, exactly? You are so simple minded!
Your crankiness screams to high heaven.
I suggest you get out your Lego set
And treat yourself. The lone wolf
In any society has to flash his teeth and
Let his god know his conscience is up for grabs.

*

8

Oh, purity of the shrill pipes and the elongated
Image of Caspar Hauser drifting into view –
Goggle-eyed sisters of mercy do trumpet solos
To make up for time lost among the thistles.

No need whatsoever to lift your knees so high,
The damage is done, the council flats shall be
Levelled to the ground, food for earthworms.
Those cantankerous fishwives will not give in.

Go outside and pray for me, I said to my wife,
I am going to tear this god-forsaken place apart.
Odysseus strode into the canteen, oh look!
They have acquainted themselves with the past.

Wisps of smoke clung, like sugary delicacies,
To Mater Delarosa's hair, she from Mexico,
Where the finches copulate for old time's sake.
So many sights to see and write home about!

When the strong man lifts up the fat woman,
Then you may guess the time of the shutdown.
When the black irises have bloomed again,
You may lift up your gaze to the sky and sing.

Promptly the lavatory ladies will dismiss their
Gigolos, polar bears will repopulate the arctic
Wastes, the value of Amazon shares will sink
Dramatically. All will be well in Disneyland.

*

9

It does seem a shame,
But no one’s to blame,
There’s an end to my life
And I don't have a wife.

So he calculated,
His ego was inflated,
The luminous stars,
The planets, Mars,

Intrigued him no end.
Was it time to transcend?
Should he care or not?
He was literally on the spot.

Out of the clouds
Streamed angelic crowds,
Completely surrounded him,
Quickly impounded him.

This serves me right, he thought.
This on myself I brought.
Oh, only look! The light
Gives me new appetite!

Time to wake up,
To drain that cup,
Oh it’s not bad.
Just a little sad.

All that comes down from there
Streams through the golden air,
Listed as special stuff,
No one can get enough.

*

10

Oh come down from your cloud and join us here.
The garden seems to sink beneath your weight.
The long forgotten tulips reappear
So innocent, as if no fear
Could weigh them down if they appeared too late.

The crocuses are absent, they remember
How last year you encouraged them to bloom
And when they blew their colours loud and clear
So innocent as if no fear
Might haunt them, oh, you seared them with your gloom.

The plum tree has been shattered, also due
To too much weight, the fruit, but half ripe, perished.
You would not join us here, we knew not why.
So innocent, as if to try
Our patience, you decried what all we cherished.

And now you keep your peace among the stars
As if it pleased you to remain within,
Indifferent to our pains, our grief and lust,
So innocent as if earth's dust
Were not to be disturbed, like rust on tin.

It seems we are condemned to think of you
As if you were a demon, without soul.
The very blood within our veins now flows
So innocent, as if, God knows,
What in our garden grows will not be whole.

*

11

Weakness, that rascal,
Comes down and scares the pants off us.
I am at last,
Like never before in the past,
Falling apart. One huge yawn
Sums up my existence.
The lesson to be learned here will be learned.

Another long yawn.
I describe this because so much else
wants to come down.
Here at the moment the truth
seems far, far away
But I know better.
I have memorized that lesson to the letter.

*

12

Icy reality, fire and brimstone,
Descends like flakes of judgment.
It takes a degree of knowhow
To deal with that sort of thing.
A crash-course in party-time,
A handful of tulips among the shards,
A penetrating wail from the heart –
What can I say, it adds up.
Still, those willows dip their golden
Branches patiently into liquid bliss.

*

13

Much happiness, when words first ride
On brindle ponies, side by side,
Along the course set out by law.
Here is where first the poet saw
The ornate garment of his art.

When out of heathen mouths the truth
Then swamped the city and the town
And drew the wrath of pope and priest
Down on unfettered brain and mind,
And when those freed souls intertwined,
Who checked the Romance of the yeast?

Kindred of lark, of spear and woe,
These simple singers of our past
Solely relied on heart's request
And out they kept a weather eye
For who would know and love them best
Before they worked and chose to die:
Fine ethos of the song was theirs.

Do we recall, now that the cloud
Of supernature has diminished us?
Will we remember that it finished us?
Out of the single moment's strength
Is furnished resurrection-glow,
Wise conception, which at length
Will double love, courage required
To see through what the muse has fired.

*

14

Thank the lord you walk and talk
While the many lie in chains,
Unable to request their escape,
Their mouths closed by duct tape.

Think how fortunate you are,
Much more fortunate by far
Than those conquerors of space
Who mislead the human race.

When it's apple blossom time
You declare your love for all
Who hang in nets like melons sweet,
With not a thing to drink or eat.

When the tiger roars at night
You despise Gemütlichkeit,
But your temper knows no bounds
As you loose those hell hounds.

Can you think your fortune true
Or is slavery your choice?
Were you once in love but cared
Little for how loved ones fared?

Oh it means a lot to me:
You're at liberty and free,
Both at once. Oh what luck!
Do you want a lollypop to suck?

No, I only need one thing
To see me through these last few years:
A golden glove, that when I touch
This modern world I will not wretch.

*

15

Terrestrial –
What is earth if not
Limitless expansion?
Whatever you choose to
Share with your greater intimacy,
Fans out to demonstrate
Endless, limitless universe.

Nothing so much
Sends me into a rage
As when someone speaks of
The age and size of the universe.
What could he possibly have in mind!
Let him track down the wolves
That have devoured his imagination.

Certainly it matters
How we imagine the truth
And the universe must not be allowed
To become a thing like so many things,
Trapped in the modern duality between
Magic and superstition, between
Ghosts and machines.

Oh, now here is another thing:
They would shrink the earth down
To the size of its critical mass,
And then they are shocked when they
Arrive at home and there is none,
And their family falls apart
Into several atoms.

*

16

Delightful messages arriving today,
Someone, somewhere is trying to say
That the origin, that which precedes all else,
Is not to be sussed. What he buys or sells

Is everyman's general, gentle behaviour
And that is where ultimately his saviour
Makes his appearance and leaves again
With no look back. When now and then

Someone with brain enough for two
Allows a double-load of goods to go through,
A thousand hosannas rise to the sky
To condense as cloud. Then, by and by,

A man looks around within his soul,
Are the windows clean, does he need more coal,
Is the front door creaking on its hinges again,
Does the roof leak? Then he picks up his pen

And writes the following: Dear Sir,
I wonder, would it ever occur
To you and yours what a great delight
It is to be alive? All else is a fight

For justice, for right, for food and shelter,
To hell and back, helter-skelter,
So I suggest you tell your people to relax
As soon as they arrive – and to cover their tracks.

*

17

Tentatively alive,
He stretched the day
To make it last.
Brutality
Tested his nerve,
Drew a crowd,
Spat in the judge's face.
Look here now,
The wrecked houses,
The flooded streets,
The poor people!

Normalization proceeds.
Covid cleans up.
Shortage of water,
Electricity off,
Down to the basics.
What are you basics?
Can you fall back on
Your hero?
Who is your hero?
A football player?
The crowd is dispersed.

*

18

Will the rain not stop?
Even outside it rains.
Danger of the dam bursting!
I am persuaded of my
Intrinsic importance to god.
Subtleties no longer
Pull any weight, do they.
The spirit of criticism
Cowers under the stairs.
Even social criticism
Is no longer social,
Only detrimental to life.

I ski down the slope
Of my iced-over emotions.
No containment policy
Succeeds under these
Horrific conditions.
Tranquilizers abound
And meanwhile the
Trains arrive on time.

The rain has stopped!
We had all agreed that
Eventually it *would* stop.
Not even a war can
Drag on forever.
The Prince's dove has died.
Now we may tell jokes
To embarrass the authorities
And walk in public in the nude.
It's a free country, ours is,
But of course there are limits.
Learn to play the flute.

*

19

Ten to one, the present moment
Is a spell and nothing counts.
May I have a little solace,
Please, it seems the grief amounts

Daily to a certain portion
Of the overall concern
And as soon as I make headway,
Ready to inquire and learn,

All those little influential
Ghosts appear and make a face.
Oh, we haven't been considered,
Our demand for time and space!

Now I limit my concession
To the sphere of human being.
Now I make my own impression,
Trusting my own hearing, seeing.

Manifold the appeal vindictive,
Plentiful the force of spite,
Gentle Jesus, hold my hand, please,
Powerful Christ, now see me right.

There are those who save their strength
For the moment when they falter.
Others, while the time seems right,
Place their gift upon the altar.

Ten to one, the present moment
Is the last at your disposal,
So you'd better make it count.
That is my sincere proposal.

*

20

Only a little believing
Deals with a lot of grieving.
God within and without
Leaves us alone, without doubt,
Until we wake up and intend
And our disbelief suspend,
For that always gets in the way
Of what all we do and say,
So that in the end we fail
And our thought is of no avail.

As soon as we fully intend
And all our dithering suspend,
Who is it stands right away
Besides us and what we say
And what we do carries weight
And our timing is never too late.
There's joy in what two do as one
And its always unique, like none,
Though we may wonder just then
What was the meaning again.

Gently the glory unfolds
Before our eyes and holds
Mystery out for those
Who behave as everyone knows.
For those who know the score,
Who part the gold from the ore,
Oh, how their works open out,
For they know what glory is about,
Namely of truth the spouse,
Beauty and truth in one house!

*

21

As many times as you may try
To stop the stream from rushing by,
It catches you and turns you round
And suddenly you feel profound.

Ideas drift past upon the shore,
You wonder were they there before
Or did they suddenly appear
When you removed yourself from fear?

A mythic animal stands proud
Upon a hill and bellows loud
When suddenly the heavens part.
What issues forth is human art.

The order of the universe
Is thought by some to be a curse
Because of their own ill-cast order,
Halfway between hate and murder.

However, much as this would cause
Us sorrow, oh, there never was
Such need for wisdom as today
When half the world is held in sway

And half is frozen tight as tight,
Political, in idealist might,
While all the swaying to and fro
Must cause a violent wind to blow.

In short, there's not much to be said
For force-the-door and slugabed
While gently-bentley all god's own
Merrily do what they've been shown.

*

22

I cannot just sit here without
Looking around with open eyes
At the totality of humanity plus
All creation on earth. That is
How I learn that within me is
Stored what it takes to be and
Also to be human.

You may count all the spirits that
Influence your behaviour and then
Choose those you know and value
Over those who tend to betray.
Let there be no trifling with gods,
For god is powerful being, love
Planted within us, without us made
Duly available as we need, as we
Want and appreciate.

That is why I leave the sequence
Of rational thought and behaviour
To merciful spirit as such, which
Includes and involves for our benefit
The impulse, the stimulus, the urge
And the painful prompt – when we
Dance or dither superstitiously or
Try to enhance our happiness as if
We alone existed.

*

The Material Earth

1

This is frightening!
Shall I ever speak again?
The tendency to let myself be carried,
Seized upon by every kind of demon.
For the purpose of demonstrating
That one exists who holds them in check,
Not to boast strength of overlordship,
No, to show to those who dare
Expertise in single-handed management
Of the powers from below.

We spread a Turkish carpet for him,
Then we practice our choral interlude,
Just in time for him to arrive, oh, such
Modesty, really the simplicity of a child
And yet power beyond all powers:
The love that rests splendidly in itself.

Time itself was magnified,
Space luminous in tandem,
You will not believe except with your
Whole heart. I suggest you test the water
Before you leap in to salvage your soul.
Can you please hold still while I drape
This soft cotton gown over your shoulders.

You will find that night will be your
Friend tonight. Unspeakable beauties linger
Where we suppose we might grasp them,
However this lotus blossom in your hair
Will have to suffice for the moment.
That canny lioness has waited for this
Moment and now it strides forth among
The cactuses in bloom and greets
The masked dancers, there where we
Met and called one another home.

*

2

Gently the rivers flow,
The streams to them contribute
Their livelier anxiety and the many
Brooks, creeks and rivulets make
Busy haste to join in the celebration.

Mountains, ranged remotely between
Sky and earth overlook the joyous occasion.
Man observes. Casts his weight behind
Each orderly progression towards
Finite ends.

In the evening of an age
New light shimmers through the chinks.
Let us make allowance for supernatural
Explanations and interpretations, they
Bend our stiff necks.

Meanwhile the high purpose
Must be made clear. We will no longer
Hesitate on this side of the crisis, dithering
For the lack of true management,
Ignoring available guidance.

But who are we? Are we
The few who run risk after risk,
Exemplifying what will not be pointed out,
Short of sleep, rushing to repair
Each crack in the dyke?

Or are we that debonair crew,
Advancing in squad cars, forcing each issue,
Alarmed when a needle is threaded
In case the priest might think
Different and punish sin?

*

3

What is it that drags us down
Against our will, our wish to limit
Experience to a scent or a smile?
Is it the fear we have of bleeding?

Will we expire if our ego is pierced?
No one demands an end to our dreaming.
Surely there is time to exaggerate our hopes,
To leap into spring at the end of winter.

Covid 19 – such an immensity of
Downright bad luck! Who would have thought
Our health was so feeble, so unexposed
To wellbeing, with all its fine securities!

Origin of life, deep in earth,
There – don't stare – the hard core
Of our timely, supernatural mercies
catches the fancy of the son of man.

Suddenly a snake exits from hiding,
Sets out on sinuous path to the sea,
Genuflects, if you can imagine that,
And the god happily negotiates a bargain.

These ruins remind me of ancient agonies,
Of enemies ever on the brink of attack.
Fumitory flourishes from between the stones
And a lone bat dreams of the moon.

*

4

Normalization processes generally adhere to
How and why we make our announcements.
As long as the acoustics stand up to these
Ultra-mundane foxes, once they begin to bark.

You see what I mean, don't you, here we
At last get up our courage to mingle with
The crowd and what do the loudspeakers
Blare in our direction? Please be seated!

Not for this did I sweat over my degrees, my
Unlimiting pulverizations of will and intellect,
Only to be cast to the wolves. Circumspect
He brought his inner powers up to the mark.

With sublime ease we may remove ourselves
From yesterday's inhibitions in favour of
Vastly more interesting contemplations today.
Try to realize, it has been accomplished for you.

Which does not imply hands in pockets or
Feet up on the desk while the boss glances
Surreptitiously through the glass partition.
Excuse me, Miss Peabody, what does it mean?

Well now, think what you owe your ancestors,
The tramped across limitless wastes to reach
Your particular gene pool, there to squat and
To drum their messages, to chant their beliefs.

*

5

There's no excuse for losing contact
And then limiting access to the cosmic cues.
Sure it takes half an hour to sit down and
Allow the various juices to concentrate.

Sometimes you'd swear nobody was home
There where the bundles of dried herbs hang
For anybody to help themselves and make no
Fuss if the spinal cord needs extra attention.

When the food arrives I stretch and say
Thank you, I couldn't do it without you.
Even at my age – or especially at my age –
The very idea of scarcity has to be ridiculed.

I stand up now and let my legs take the weight
Of two-thousand years of tragic modernity.
It feels great. What all goes on down there
Will soon be revealed to the public gaze.

For one thing, our roof will soon need to be
Rethatched. It's the kind of thing you don't
Think of while the party-goers are rounded up
In the public square for the Home Secretary.

That much said, the cross-channel swimming,
Which was cut short so that homing pigeons,
Which had strayed, might sort out their
Sat-navs, shall proceed with gov't support.

When all is said and done, there is, under-
standably, nothing left to do or say, unless
We check in the attic, among all the plunder,
Is there any chance of compassionate suffering?

*

6

Difficult to say how far we have to travel
Before we realize we stand on earth
For a reason and for a purpose. Our joy
Eliminates all emotions when we understand
How far the stars are from one another,
So that no one is able to remove himself
From his humanity. Nonetheless many try.
This is the puzzle of the modern age, that
Wherever we look the bonds are broken.
The waters no longer wash us clean and
The fires no longer warm us except to inform
Mind and soul of flesh and blood presence.

If we rise high enough, we will not be forced
Down – such food for thought! If we speed
To a certain degree we will be unable to slow
Down. I address this to extinct Scientists.
The non-rotation of the earth must alert us
To the stationary confrontation of our soul
With god who is not a god. That which rests
In itself loves Maya and daily unites with
Such endeavours as we are urged to undertake.
No control of life here. All imaginable law
Shall not be traduced, however love acts
All-powerfully, here and now, earth-bound.

*

7

Erstwhile, when the clock still ticked,
And the broad band of crimson illuminations
All along the eastern sky sang beautifully,
My love and I were wont to bestow our approval.
Arm in arm we sauntered along the ocean's edge
While dark-eyed seals played among the waves.

We knew nothing then of what was to come
On account of worldwide poor housekeeping.
We only felt the moment's rich promise.
However soon large tracts of land subsided,
Lava bubbled from the granite king's nostrils,
The fine technique of termites was interrupted.

Nowadays some lean in the direction of sickness
While scavenger toads mate in nearby slums
And none dare suss the dire disconnect of things.
My love and I peruse our schoolroom books,
Content in adjacent attics above the tenements,
While our foot-soles touch and we smile.

*

8

Mining the human reality
For element substance leaves
Hardcore for popular consumption
Which I take in stride, accustomed
As I am to the literal function.

Some would object to this
All but violent measure
But look to the times, my friend.
Not everyone sees how close we were
Yesterday to the end.

There, for but one example,
The shirts were drying on the line
When the moon rang out
Loud and clear above the noise
Made by the popular shout.

Trial by dirt and saliva
Produces that knock-on effect
For which our soldiers have trained
And we can't wait to cut loose
The ground our poets have gained.

Plate full of mash, a sausage
Dipped in the blood of Christ,
What, for God's sake, does it mean,
That with all his scientific nuance
The man can't recall what he's seen?

*

9

I'm sorry, but you're going to have to
Rethink it all over again. The folk tune
Smashes the plates on the kitchen floor
And dances barefoot on the shards,
Takes a selfies and gets out the cards.
All this goes on irrespective of what
TS Eliot did or thought or Stravinsky
Scooped from the barrel out back.
Strictly speaking, there's no lack
Of anecdotal jelly or jam.
If you're the man, take strides
That suit your orbicular backdrop –
Winnie the Pooh is always watching,
So ponder the tricks played by fate.

It's snowing outside this Sunday morning
I can tell from the tracks on the footpath
That Pat from next door has been out and in.
There's kindness in the air, children
Are not allowed out because of the Covid,
He slinks behind walls, crawls among bushes
Ready to pounce. The grown-ups all look
For what isn't there. We know it's inside
And there we let it abide. It's organic.
Let it ride, Granny! Remember, in your day,
They tried to make the bad guys go away
By calling them names? Those times
Are over. Don't judge the poem by its
Rollicking rhythm or rhyme. Judge your self.

*

10

In front of me the gradual dissolution,
Behind me rabbit tracks in the snow.
Who would argue with the world today?
Has so-called tradition still anything to say?
No, we live in seclusion, each one of us,
Barely aware of a common light ray.

Sure, we can read in books how it once was,
Out there, I mean, and how a few blithe spirits
Stared knowingly into the darkness,
Undismayed when private tragedy struck.
Is it really true that they realized
That nothing, not a thing, could be done
To avert the truth from the world?
That nations should unite with other nations
To discuss the regression of the truth,
Then to do final battle against those with
Other method, schemes, of falsehood?

The universal giddiness is surely a good sign.
Does anyone really care what happens outside?
Indeed, what could it possibly mean that
Something should still happen outside?
Why was illusion ever imagined as reality?
And then illusion was discarded altogether,
Well, what did you expect, in your cave?
This is what crossed my mind tonight
As I reflected upon the earth's spirit and
How it might renew itself, in heart's ease.

*

11

It occurs to me that I should be
Making room for the younger generation,
However, when it comes to that, I have
Not actually occupied space anyone else can use.
With that in mind, I shall hang on to the glorious end.
It's not as if nothing were left to do. Good grief,
I have merely scratched the surface!
I have indicated, merely indicated, what for the
Lack of a better word I call true reality.
Not that this was my own idea.
In fact it was no idea at all.
This, I feel, needs to be accentuated.
If the film had been peeled back abruptly,
Oh, can you imagine the sorry display
Of sensitive flesh without skin?

Down there, where the bills of a thousand storks
Have broken through the earth's crust
To release children that have waited, waited,
The first-arrivals stretch, blink in the red sun,
Perform the dance then, meaning: I can't believe
How long it took, Sully, to get the place ready!
And the earth closes for another little while.
Remembrance is staged, like old men's protests
Now and again: For Christ's sake, don't ignore us!
The children bathe their feet in puddles of rain water.
It gives them something to do while they
Wait for the curtain to be dawn back. Then:
Noises off! – Oh dear, do you call that an audience?
Bring on the bloke who was hired to advertise.
Mind you now, there's no cause for gloom.
It's not up to us to call the shots.

*

12

Not by a long stretch
Will the one who for years has tackled
Every annoyable weakness of man and woman,
Continue to bring his testation to bear
On those who are neither here nor there
But wrapped in cosmic occlusion.

They are the ones we look out for,
Yet, all the same, based on illusion,
Trending like salmon towards birthplace,
They remain in majestic mood and configuration,
Exchanging outward for inward station
While we hold our breath and wait.

Carefully numbering paragraphs, pages
Of the book of life, we continue
To organize all that lends itself
To the thin-skinned, perceptive touch of a hand
Without losing manner or means in the sand,
For that is our will-power.

It never occurred to us
How at last they might soar overhead, indifferent
To brain and breath of our hidden efforts,
To all we managed to coin and control,
The hidden taxes, payment of toll –
Now they kick over the traces and burn bridges?

*

13

Oh look! It's the lyrical eye,
Come for a visit. What is it?
Can we be of service, we who
Organize yellow, green and blue
Into some self-centred deposit
Of reality based on itself here?

I see the lyrical eye and believe
The universe not in a box but
Those who tremble under the weight
Of their time, obscure, second-rate,
thus annexed, blown like ash,
no excuse necessary.

Oh look, it's the mile-high club,
Assembling to compare notes.
Suddenly the mountain looms,
Final words for brides and grooms.
The exact measure is demanded,
Some are worthy, some burn.

What clubs together is massive,
Straw, molecular, the split.
Then the witnesses assemble,
Some observe them and tremble,
Station upon station falls,
And the soft voice calls.

*

14

Oh, good grief! When will I learn
That the thousand things are not mine to earn.
What is it that happens to me when I think
If I start to write I won't have enough ink,
If I tremble before the word of god,
This must be due to god's merciless rod?

The least increment of desuetude felt,
Of loneliness experienced, of friendship withheld,
Of lack of recognition for services rendered
Unwilling acceptance of solutions tendered,
Cold-hearted rejection of myself as wise –
Upsets me, causes my gorge to rise.

Now I suppose it really shouldn't matter
How I react when people scatter
As soon as I enter a room on my own.
After all I'm mature, more than half grown
Towards the end of my days on earth without end.
When the pain sets in, I can always transcend.

I know how to suffer whatever pain
Or inconvenience drives me half insane.
I have learned how to duck when arguments fly
Like stones in my vicinity and by an by
I will even make a habit of asking for joy
When I'm made to feel like an ignorant little boy.

*

15

Onwards, onwards the earth turns
Under our feet, we can barely keep up.
Right away the galaxies speak up,
We too, we too wish to be noticed.
So much light is reflected off these hills,
Such a tumult of sheep on that meadow,
Where to we start, where can we start?

There is no beginning whatsoever and
We might as well make up our mind –
Which task is readily accomplished
If we choose to submit to wild things –
That among the stars there are spaces
Inhabited by empires on continents
Classically defined as germ-free.

Neither, when it comes to that, is there
An end, especially not where you would
Expect one among those oak tree roots,
Tangled in subsoil, mutually affectionate.
Ends and beginnings enclose death,
Let us make a habit of speaking softly of
Death and of its undetrimental face like

That of a mist-drenched daisy in bloom.
Oh look, we have stepped across that
Stile as though heaven were attuned to
Us and our ancestors, so it seems, and
Willingly I would empty all my book
Shelves into the arms of a demigod,
If such a one were to sup with me.

Alas, the purple emperors dance in the
Crown of that oak as if all hell had
Broken loose and they were in charge.
It must be their mating season. They
Blunder belligerent into the finches.
There is no end, no beginning and
My heart goes out to those who flee.

*

16

Calm the lake, its surface shimmers,
Oh, the tribal chiefs plan war.
Now the jungle drums fall silent,
Tensed, we hear the lions roar.

In a minute we are tested –
Is our courage up to par,
But an hour has sixty minutes
And we wait – our goal is far.

Sanctioned by tradition's blunders,
Trimmed to shape by fear and pain,
Well aware of foolish habits,
Our desires must keep us sane.

Though we love, to fit occasion,
Though we suffer to remove
Many of our past transgressions,
Destiny has carved its groove.

Diligent each day's endeavours,
Timely aided by repair,
What was sanctioned by the nation.
Now it takes us to the fair.

Clabbered by post-modern nonsense,
On false oceans set adrift,
Shake yourself, imagine truly,
gentle spirit requires a lift.

Torn by fury stand the branches
Out into the midnight sky.
Now we wait and let good angels
Lead our caravanserai.

*

17

A few snow flurries,
Cold as hell and
Life itself is a contradiction.
To trump it all
One has to buy a newspaper,
Otherwise the world's end
Will sneak up on us and
Take us by surprise.

Within, everything is clear.
The wombats are munching,
The gravel is crunching
And where the statue of God stood
A penguin is gulping a herring.
Many street signs have been reversed,
So that now when we wish to
Go to the hairdresser's

We end up saying our prayers.
I recall Dorothy Sayers
Saying to us students
That the monkish life is not
Worth a continental, whereupon
I had to ask what a continental is.
She laughed and said:
"Where have you lived?"

Since then I got the drift.
Even the houses wear masks now
And unless something shows
Evidence of hardship
It gets discarded. As for people,
They are learning new songs
And most of them by now can
Speak English and knit jumpers.

*

18

A new foothold gained,
A sort of justification for
Cosmic anger plus deadly nightshade,
And if you want to clap your hands,
Go right ahead. All plants are listening.

Meagre sport, this group therapy,
The heady humour of the viruses;
Slade stands back, reserved, it
Comments on the vivacity of a mole.
Look there, an open brook!

Calisthenics to keep anything alive
Are no longer necessary.
Is this really the hand that
Clawed its way up cliffs and stroked
The buttocks of that maid?

You can put it any way you like,
No one is listening. The graves
are gaping, those wild scientific illusions
have been scraped off the sky.
Look now, here it is!

Are you afraid of a little tergiversation?
Has your candle burnt down and now
The moths no longer struggle on the
Tablecloth? I recall vividly
How once you insisted on love of life.

Make me happy, she said and I laughed.
Then she laughed and we embraced.
The thousand things
No longer clings
And everywhere the birdies sings.

*

19

Beset by earth spirits,
Devoid of all liveliness
We must find tangible relief
Or else concentrate on a work in hand.
The brightness of this present day
Would teach us all we have forgotten,
Would limit our liberty to a single point.
No wonder we have difficulty embracing
The full meaning of our purpose here.

Song within the tree trunks,
Song under the prairie's
Fragrant, element-rich surface,
Voices beckoning – those least conscious
Of dream-meaning speak the final truth
And feed it into sun, water and fire, thereby
Ensuring many cosmic completions.
This anguish I carry with me down these
Strenuous streets will ripen to fruition.

This is the narrow point,
The tight place where root
And stem meet to transport life's
Pressing immediacy upwards and outwards.
You may well look for the name that will
Sum this up but you will fail until you
Search within self for nameless, personal
Identification, human being itself,
Never allowed to be wasted.

*

20

Why should deep, deep down
Be any different from high, high up?
This has been known for many years
And we might as well look at it again.
In your eyes, for example, I see
Breakers crushing seaweed against cliffs
While my heart snoozes in a fine peace.
Consider these two as very much the same.
Or you finally part from me in a mad rush
While I feel a blend of anxiety and relief.
Should we comb the beach for sea stars?
Should I pick your pocket for a diamond?
Oh it has just now occurred to me that
All those people on the subway are
Even lonelier than I am, which brings
Tears to my eyes and memories to my mind.
We allowed ourselves to be guided by
The wind and by gifts of roses, by harsh
Comments and by tiny speckled fishes.
Eventually we give up because at last
We realize that nothing is to be done.
Sunbeams are the same as moonbeams
And a violent gesture sets off a dream.
Horrible cars along the straight highway
Are so uncompassionate, so 'driven' by
Yesterday's pains, by ancient sickness,
That all I can think of is a little girl
Running barefoot up a mountain trail
Until she spots a porcupine on a tree.
There she sits now and I apologize.

*

21

The ancient mass, when nothing drew attention
Yet to the truth or to its offspring, rests within
Our indecisive souls, yet to be quarried
For the purpose of present day exactitude
And here we present the amorphous platitudes:

Diatribes en masse, not to be avoided,
Kingfisher-blue magic tricked out for
Subconscious consumption, to mislead,
If possible, the angry farmer, the wise child.
Also you immerse yourself in its foul energy.

Oh, if the Greeks had known! (Who are they?)
Oh, if the Romans had known, when they
Capitulated to the grim usurpers, that hell
Energizes and fucks up outer space!
Who, exactly, are 'the Romans'? Who knows.

Down here is absolutely no relation,
No degree and no difference. This is the
Universalist option, take it or leave it, but
Know that it depends on you whether you
Thrive or go down like the rest of the age.

Gentle Jesus needs no heroes to placate
The modern artifice, needs merely to look,
To absorb, to send out flyers, advertising
In-house management of all the dung which
Fortifies, oh yes, make no mistake, dear!

Finally all is cleared up and we smile, because
Now 'crucifiction' and 'reserection' evaporate,
Then settle in the valleys of the foothills where
Enigmatic gold lies buried, which we always
Knew, but now we experience truth as weight.

*

22

All that is large and impressive
Comes from the earth in its time.
Never mistake the progressive
Fall from grace as a climb.

Think how you lift the unnerving
Experience as though you respected
The way you avoid by swerving
Only to find you're protected.

Then as the calcification
Threatens corpuscle and cell,
Dedication works unification
And you thrive,
for you might just as well.

*

23

If it were known
That all this is really our own,
We would no longer speculate
Or drive our functions to the limit.

Third-hand resurrection is no longer
Advertised, however this means
That the soft soap no longer cleans
Our soul of health and happiness.

None of us are worried.
We have been ferried
To the other side pronto.
Some walked, some were carried.

*

24

Comes a time to play
No matter what.
Comes a time to say
Just what matters today
And wipe them away,
The tears that rot.

You look out for me
All day and night.
Why could we not be
Absolutely free,
Like a bird, a bee,
With no more spite?

Comes a time to throw
Caution to the winds.
Comes a time to know
Beginnings and ends
And all that time sends,
The unexpected woe.

In the end we feel
That no end lasts.
All things that appeal
Cannot be real.
Only beings heal,
Not plaster casts.

Stand narrow and straight
As if life were space
and you a figure of eight
dancing till late.
Spit in the eye of fate
And heaven embrace.

*

25

Undisturbed, the sickness lasts
But the grace of god disturbs.
Even if the patient fasts,
Medication, tinctures, herbs
Will not help him if he drifts
Where the egotist holds court,
Using spirit as a tool.
Every effort will abort.
Slavish sex becomes the rule
As the male insists on conquest
And the female hides her pride.
In the end there's lack of interest
While god's grace is pushed aside.

Faith as energy suffices
To install the gift of grace.
Helpful hindrance once or twice is
No mistake in time and space
While the soul remains intact,
Flesh and spirit, each to each,
So much more than just familiar,
Mercy's function within reach.

When once more the ego conquers,
Meaning, that it bites its tail
And a thousand little terrors
Have been scotched to no avail,
Best to linger where the wounded
Self replenishes its source
Of intestine saturation
While the misery runs its course.
Every monkey knows this wisdom,
Every elephant, lion or mouse,
Only humans are rejected;

Which is why we're resurrected,
Every husband and his spouse,
Every friend and his companion
Where true love has forged the link
And where genius with its mysteries
Drives the elements to the brink.

Never have I been so thwarted
As when under pain's duress
I have forced my issue forward
In the hope of quick redress.
For we grow at speeds we know not
But we grow, and that's a fact,
Once we've stated our intention.
There's one more thing I would mention:
Inequalities attract,
Not just opposites. We linger,
We suppose we merely drift;
We despise, we fear, we're tempted,
None of god's own are exempted,
Then we're ready for the gift.

All this, just to be accepted,
Hopefully not cast aside.
Next time when we look around us
All the doors are open wide
And the love the gods would lavish
On our self and on our soul
Dwindles, for our god would ravish
All his children, sane and whole.
Entertained, we step out lively,
Kindred spirits, one and all.
If we only knew this early
We could do without the fall,
We would practice, daily, yearly.

*

26

So you have a moment free,
You decide to think of me,
And I share our understanding;
In the square the planes a landing.

What you do is wishful thinking,
Superstitions interlinking,
Troubled heart, uncertain mind;
Now your taste shall be refined.

Goodness me, the birds are singing,
Can you hear the churchbells ringing?
Let our peace go out to others;
Choose your sisters and your bothers.

Now be ready for some changes,
While the spirit rearranges.

*

27

It occurs to me that I need help.
I reach out to where in the past
The spirit of life has entrusted itself
To the one I was at that time under
Circumstances nothing like those
Which at present encumber me.

Not that I have to prepare myself
For some particular attention I seek,
No, it suffices that I present myself
As I am at that particular moment,
Slightly confused perhaps or in pain.
Mainly the next step forward has

Seemed incredibly difficult for me
Even though I feel constrained to act.
So the question I ask is: What now?
I accompany this with a note of
Regret for having behaved badly –
Well, I must have, isn't it obvious?

The underlying repentance is surely
Essential, as I experience frequently,
When sheer willpower alone causes
More problems rather than solving
Those that have arrived on my plate.
I wonder, does this need to be said?

When the response arrives, as it has
Always done in the past, I am changed.
I no longer see myself as I did when
I asked for help and also the world
Itself has changed, generally now for
The better, and the next step is easy.

* * * * *

The Endless Universe

1

But if we cannot reflect,
Only to sect and intersect
And if the noises draw all things
Down to the level of that
Fine mesh stretched between
Whipsnade and causality,

Where will it all end?
For those who wish to transcend
The curtain readily is drawn
Aside while the public leaves.
Thank you, Mrs. Hilton,
Your flowers are much appreciated.

Life these days is a going
Concern and I cannot imagine
Why we should not keep free of
Each and every sinkhole in
The neighbourhood, after all
These are knotty problems.

They make for the sort of music
That bottles up atmosphere
And creates distinct illusion.
They announce happenstance
Occurrences such as the headless
Horseman riding to Banbury.

This trifling matter of the truth
Has once again lifted the lid
On sections of history where
The albatross of ancient lineage
Is slaughtered for public consumption
While an elephant smirks.

*

2

No one cares how much I suffer,
Which is just the way I like it.
I would, you know, get entangled
In fronds of seaweed down there.
No, I lap my milk from a saucer
And then stand aside of the world's
Transactions that flay the population.

All this aside, however, pay no
Attention to the diggers in the town
Centre. A grave has been upheaved
Where for years unidentified fumes
Had risen from brown apertures
In the earth's thin skin. A grave,
Now, can mean only one thing:

At this precise spot, in the year when
Antiquity turned modern – yes,
You'd not been aware of that, had you –
Five elephants lifted the earth on their
Shoulders and marched towards –
Oh dear! I've forgotten the name of it.
It's all a matter of ancient writ.

Bouncing onto the screen suddenly
From behind where roses have
Bloomed for centuries, the clown –
I mean a particular clown now –
Untangles the snakes that have
Constricted his act so immoderately
And the luminescence nearly blind us.

*

3

Does it surprise you that I can
Draw forth from the earth's centre
All these universal explanations?
That is because you have agreed
To be fashioned in the example of
The ubiquitous machine.

Now you must allow yourself to be
Bundled cocoon-wise for the interim.
What do I mean by the interim?
You ask too many questions instead of
Letting my words do their secret work.
Finish what you are doing now.

The home crowd is still applauding
The performance not because the
Players gave their all – they did not –
But because the home team won.
You see how it goes, don't you. When
All is said and done, the buck stops.

I include a resurrection motif.
There is no accounting for style.
The celluloid buckles under the hammer.
Too much is being taken for granted
These days and always has been,
My grandmother knew it and said so.

Now you may offer your own gift.
Lay it there upon the altar.
Now remove yourself from the premises
Before the priests decide to worship
The ground you stand on. They have
Acquired the most obnoxious habits.

*

4

There's no gratitude from those with
Cotton between the ears, that goes
Without saying. All along the star-
spangled horizon the great liners and
The container ships compete for space.

Space, you see, is the essential service
And those who rush out into it in the
Hope of transfiguration need their
Nails clipped and their ears cuffed
Because they spoil it for the rest of us.

The financial market brings peace
To the minds of those who dance to the
Tunes of outlandish orchestras while
Flat-footed orangutans try to rule
The earth as though it meant something.

You can never say you are finished
While a single drop of blood pulses
In any of your arteries or veins.
I like to come up with a complete
Picture of the universe on fire.

Salted herring in the sky with diamonds
And a hard rain landing on daft
Critters who wouldn't be worth
Sending against the professional
Socialists – it's what I'm up against.

*

5

Suddenly the universe petered out
And the earth's populations were
Outraged, would you blame them?
While a single bluebottle still rattles
Inside the Chinese lampshade I will
Insist on my right to complain against
These tight-lipped provocations.

Here we stand, a veritable army,
Dedicated to the configuration of the
Cosmos as we experience it now,
And no one has the right to tell us
To go home and lick our wounds.
Suddenly the earth opens and our
Enemies are swallowed in one gulp.

We are the activists and we insist
On our right to smash you to
Smithereens, don't you know, and
There's nothing you can legally do
To stop us or to make us behave.
We may not know what we mean
But then that's not the point, is it

The things is, that god has plans for me
That I cannot fathom ahead of time.
This has to be understood properly,
Not through a tube of glass or plastic.
I am merely the one whose own wishes
Are put on the back burner until the
Time come for me to roast my lamb.

So many catastrophes are foretold and
Many come forward to help them along,
Which makes me wonder should I maybe
Prepare for the time when the lid
Blows off and the soup hits the ceiling?
Come to think of it, I have been doing
Just that for the past fifty years and more.

*

6

There, look, I am pointing
At distant stars which are close
In comparison to those more distant
And then I shut my eyes and imagine
That much that begets distance resides
In the pupil of my eye.

We cannot imagine ourselves
Free of the hunger for freedom
Or captivated by endless liberty.
Best to succumb to our liberated
Human nature, however distant still
From our daily lucubrations.

If a spider were to subject itself
To our intrigued scalpel, would we
Leap at the chance of killing for life,
Or was that a modern notion, outworn
Now beyond all recognition by our
New eye accustomed to solicitude?

It must eventually come to fruition,
This perpetual drumbeat of the heart,
For we long for our own heart,
We have had a taste of sanctity and
Now we long for the flesh and blood,
To be rid of the malformed ideas.

So cook me personally a meal
That will help me forget that I ever
Met you, critical spirit like dirt still
Under my nails, though, to be fair,
How would we have got on without
Your prodding, cancerous reminders?

*

7

Transmit as much as you can
Of the beauty that reaches out to you,
Why else would it stay with you?
Your familiarity with lilac and crocus
Plus yesterday partly recalled and
At long last remembered, these
Amount to a single life stream
Upon which you may sail through the day.
Certainly no one has the right
To alter your circumstances just because
They do not suit his wild dreaming.

That much said, we turn to the here and
Now, so that time and space may merge –
Which is not likely to happen suddenly.
Nothing lets you pull it apart,
Everything insists upon propriety,
Pancakes appear on the table and the
Guests arrive in droves to partake
Of this sudden, fresh arrangement.
You keep looking in my direction
As if you could not quite believe what your
Eyes see, in short, what your body registers.

The clacking of teeth, the thumping of
Elbows on the tablecloth, fat wiped off
Fingers and lips, chairs scraped back –
The meal is in progress because we
Say that it is, for in reality it has no
Will of its own such as a cult meal,
Which would draw our attention to
Here and now, time and space finally healed.
Tendencies take longest to fall into place,
Climbing boots clinging to scraps of flint,
Perspiration thick on a pony's flank.

*

8

Never tire yourself out.
Wait for the goods to arrive,
Set traps, send out invitations,
All this is fine and dandy
And takes no toll. Nerves are racked
By insistence upon the particular
That cannot even be imagined!
Yes, I barely exaggerate. We do see,
In certain places, areas, localities,
Driftwood gathered en masse,
Perpetual crops planted as if the earth
Might be repopulated as it was
Before the calamity struck.
I praise all those efforts, for without praise,
The common human heart collapses
In a heap, eventually, dragged down
By supposed hardships in themselves of
No real importance or value.

This spring-loaded little gizmo which I
Recently acquired for a pittance from
The internet, would you believe, has
Amazing properties, as ever so many
People have discovered who trusted their luck.
Input? Sex energy. That's what it says on the
Instruction leaflet that came along in the package.
Constructed from whippoorwill feathers and
Low-calorie milk product, it fits
Neatly to the tip of your willpower,
Whereupon all you do is wait quietly for
Historicity to bite. I have known
People with a persecution complex cured
Almost immediately. Of course there's a snag.
You have to know what you're doing,
Else the apparatus fails and
You yourself are blamed for the failure.
Oh, for shame! Best think twice.

*

9

Downtown the bells are ringing,
Cars are parked on the footpaths,
I wish I lived somewhere else,
The perception of freedom in this town
Is ancient, to say the least. Take the
Following: Three horsemen galloped down
Main Street shouting abuse at
Utterly well-behaved pedestrians.
Now under normal circumstance I would say
This is to be expected these days.
Look at the newspapers. Look in the mirror.
Change is due, I know, but heretofore
We were duly warned before the axe came down.

Ach well, no use complaining.
They are running out of body bags at the leisure centre.
Police, ambulance and circus performers have
Joined forces to make the unexpected more predictable.
The judges have this wing-ding method of
Expediting convictions by bribing the witnesses.
I say, power to them. Everybody is guilty.
If they grabbed me off the street I'd say:
No argument from me, boys, I must have done it some time.
Well that's the thing, isn't it, you like to help out.

National security is another problem.
You can no longer rely on the Russians to be enemies,
So you have to persuade them a little.
The worst is always this feeling of
Endlessness, of not being able to
Buckle down to some particular defence against
The enemy within or without.
People can be heartless. Here they have
All the time in the world to be happy
And what do they do? Exactly!

*

10

Universal suffering is such a blessing!
There was a time when you couldn’t vote
Unless yer Da was a foreman at the coalmine.
I suffer most days and I try to do it gladly.
I dutifully keep my complaints on ice
And concentrate on tight gaskets and oiled hinges.
The wife is hankering for a holiday again
But I say to her: Let your entire day be a holiday.
Enjoy your work. Be kind to the neighbours.
You have to keep a tight reign on the female
And only the woman can do it, it’s well known.

As for me, I join the boys at the pub. Not many
Actual men around these days. Not since Manchester
Lost five nil to Liverpool. Salah’s the exception.
Klopp too. Now there’s a man after me own heart.
Always cheerful, fair-minded, excellent teeth –
As you’d expect from a German among foreigners.
Actually I think the Germans won the war,
I mean in real terms. What was I saying?

Ah yes. We used to be able to buy our bread at the
Supermarket. Now we have to bake it ourselves.
And you know why that is, don't you. The midges.
It all started with the midges. People used to shout:
“Here come the midges!” for a joke, like, until they
Realized what was happening. This holy man –
Well, he came into our town and after a while
No one was able to claim for sick leave.
So they tarred and feathered him. Fair play!

I’m not saying that the times are getting worse.
It’s just that you can’t get a cheap hamburger anymore.
Oh, and the price of stamps has gone up too.

*

11

The brain was empty,
Then the ghosts moved in.
He drew up a list of complaints –
And threw it in the bin.

Our salad days are over, friends,
The summer will be hot and long.
Today there's music in the square,
There's revelry, there's dance and song.

Then the head was vacant.
The ghosts had been ejected.
We refused the insurance money,
We want to be resurrected.

There's no more walking on the grass,
The laws are being tightened.
Bears are roaming in suburbia;
We're not frightened.

Next came the heart.
The devil had left a mess.
Now the damage has been done
And it's too late to confess.

Tie a hanky to a stick,
Wave it and shout: What ho!
Get some rotted horse manure,
It makes the tulips grow.

Finally the genitalia –
At last, all spic and span!
Ready for whatever comes next.
First phone your Gran'.

I think we've done our level best
To get this far at least half sane.
In order to prepare for love and fresh air
It's best to start with your brain.

*

12

From where I sit I can see
Clouds gathering over the town,
Then drifting off, to the north,
Leaving behind a clear, blue sky.

I recall hiking in the Rockies,
Alone or with friends,
Up behind the Three Sisters or in
Larch Valley, beside Mt. Temple.

In those days solitude reigned,
Lake O'Hara lay peaceful,
Skirted by trails well tended by
Grassi who lived in his log cabin.

I fished in Lake McArthur and
Hiked up the flank of Mt. Biddle
With Michael, but it rained and
We returned to our tent.

I recall leaping in great bounds
Down the long scree slope between
Mt. Babel and the Tower of Babel.
Moraine Lake shimmered nearby.

Leonard Leacock, my piano teacher
Introduced me to the mountains.
On weekdays we hiked and on
Sundays he taught me harmony.

I don't get lost in those memories.
They are with me as reminders
Of a youth well spent and of
Friends still with me in spirit.

*

13

When the sky fills with blood
And people pray to be heard,
Can we take that to mean one thing:
Law and order are no sanctuary?

When some people get it into their minds
That their hero's words must not be challenged,
Death stands nearby and snicker;
This is death negative and elemental.

What if a mind is schooled for a lifetime
To think of law as an ideal
And of human flesh and blood as dispensable?
Is anything possible other than chaos?

People who choose other people as leaders
Are surely asking for the worst of trouble.
Think – what has divided you against yourself?
What makes a man choose a king for himself?

Lies piled upon lies when emotions rage
And passions drive the blood to an otherwise
Empty brain, a head devoid of judgment.
Not merely sight but the very light is put out.

Let us help those who cannot help themselves to
Acquire a degree of reflection and self-knowledge.
Let us persuade those whose good sense has been
Spoiled and unfounded, to draw breath correctly.

None, when born, are incapable of learning
Kindness and self-respect, but the brain sleeps,
So that all manner of evil takes root and the head
Is possessed by infernal ideals and instruction.

*

14

The tendency to cry out
When the pain accumulates
Rather than gently ebbing away
Is perfectly understandable
But there's no need to make a meal of it.
Everybody is hurting somewhere.
Going out in the fresh air helps.
Also you might meet someone who says:
"How are you doing today?" and
Although you will feel like saying:
"How am I doing what?" you will
Give him the benefit of your understanding.
You will tell him exactly where it hurts
And for how long it has been hurting
And how you feel about that. You will
Tell him that you are the victim of
Other peoples insensitivity and no matter
How much you knock yourself out,
Where's the appreciation these days, eh?

Well now, he will thank you for giving him
The opportunity to sympathize with you
And although secretly he despises you,
He will overcome that reaction in himself.
Then he will explain that you have
Misunderstood him. All he meant was:
'Hello, shall we tell one another a few lies?'
So when you came out with the truth
And awkwardly at that, not even with
sufficient fellow feeling, he was shocked.

Actually, when we advertise our pain,
This has nothing to do with the truth,
Only with the fact that we are at the end of
Our tether and we don't care about anyone else.
This is also perfectly understandable.

*

15

Is it absolutely necessary
That I feel the way I do?
There are so many ways to feel.
Why can I not feel as I wish?

The dreams that storm us,
That overwhelm our body and soul,
Leave a great variety of tracks
And we should make use of them.

Anyhow, that's how I feel about it.
So I impinge upon my various pains.
After locating them I respectfully
Ask them to reveal to me their origin.

Usually the response is: Dreams.
Now I know that my dreams visit me
For this one particular reason:
They wish to be told to others.

Certainly I shall not describe images.
I long for the dream substance, not its
Traces on the skin of my brain
Where at present they pester me.

Gone are the days of haruspication,
Of learning the value of what is
From what seems. Of delving into
Garbage dumps for the crown jewels.

I have in mind a leisurely conquest of
My future while it hangs in the air –
Of the past before the moths attack,
Of my psyche before it struts its stuff.

Actually I would like to find a way
To allow my dreams to reveal themselves
Without interference from me and
Solely as additives to the light of day.

*

16

Never you mind now,
You have enough to be getting on with,
The country is being run by those who
Have the nerve for it and the mandate.
Why would you hesitate before making
A single decision? Row your boat
Close to the shore and you will capsize,
You may almost take that for granted.

Such was the advice given to me when
First I entertained the notion of becoming
A human being, human throughout.
Today I realize that at the time I did
Not know how high the stakes were but
When you've stood in the mud all you life,
A square metre of hard ground, of dry land,
Takes your breath away and you say: Yes!

So for me it was Yes, emphatically.
Then I heard the drawbridge go up
And I realized there was no going back.
When that happens you reflect for a moment
Simply because you had not counted on that.
Sure, if it gets rough you can turn around –
But not so. That much came home to me.
So I decided to make that break in myself too.

Then, gradually, the help was piled on.
Good spirit guided, encouraged and comforted.
My true nature was revealed to me: this was
Perhaps the single most useful bit of
Knowledge that came my way, because now
Every move I make will be recorded
And made available to all who had the
Sense to take an interest and to take part.

*

17

To be well past the age when emotions
Crowd the soul, drawing it to attention,
The half-baked, inattentive thing;
Once it was honoured by the beasts
And another time the bleached thing
Tolerated the company of theologians.

To be no longer annoyed by the absent-
mindedness of the hill dwellers who
Leaped to attention at the mention of
War for what was to be gained there,
Namely development. It never ceased
To knock at the door of the young ones.

Now to seek the company of rowdies
In high positions too, star-gazers with
Something to answer for to a woman,
To children in splendid attire on a
Sunday outing to church or circus,
It's mostly all the same for most now.

To wait, perhaps, at the roadside here
For the man with the loaded bicycle,
Trinkets we women craved because
Otherwise what we laughingly called
Our lives were a drugged passage in
Darkness, where guilty eyes glared.

In the end an immense catastrophe,
Finally seen through, and the hillsides
Closed over many an unknown grave.
Thus, to be glad to have suffered
And eager to leap into creative action,
The limbs flexing, the eyes sparkling.

*

18

Of course one supposes that there is
Justice just around the corner, however
Justice is not what we want but to be
Judged that we're right. Illusions
Drop on our doorstep and we choose
To allow ourselves to be affected.
Is this not exactly how it should be?
What we take in is surely not what we
Give out again. Or is it? Well, one may
Toy with one's perception of the overall
Apparatus, political, media, conscience
And then return safe and sound to one's
Beloved family. Or may one? Sadly,
There are questions on both sides and
The middle traditionally escapes us.

The question is, whom do we blame for
Our accumulating bad luck, our ill health,
The fact that so many seem happier than
We would ever have the gall to be? What?
Sorry. Something unexpected crept in.
Dollars and cents, pounds and pence,
Or a bit of change jingling in our pockets –
Suddenly we stand naked in front of
Our selves, would you believe, and
Good spirit literally has no evidence
That we exist now or have ever existed.
At the time, sadly, we cannot even make
That comparison. I have been there,
I know, believe me – or don't, carry on
Trusting what other people think of you.

*

19

Suddenly my evolution, if I may put it
In a manner befitting, has other plans.
Pain sets in where I cannot identify it
And then I deal with panic and doubt.

What weakness means is known to me
And all too often I do not act accordingly.
Meanwhile the universe, its endless refrain,
Instead of entertaining, drives me insane.

Perhaps I shall draw up a list of all things
That incriminate my evolutionary growth.
On the other hand, the initial fault lies
With my silly efforts to do it all myself.

Cooperation with creative spirit remains
The one single recipe for renewed success.
So here now I have arrived at a conclusion
That should see me trough this impasse.

Some are set out, from youth, in the hills
With their ankles pinned together and
Whoever finds them may not always know
How to go about bringing them to freedom.

Eventually, however, the initial purpose
Of their sorry captivity will come to light.
Then the very delusion of freedom which
Reigns in that country must reveal itself.

Cooperation with merciful good spirit is
Of the essence in our time and we do well
To take that to heart as soon as possible or
We will be blown off our perch in the end.

*

20

Anger crashes out into the environment.
What's going on today? What is happening?
Are we being visited by insuperable odds?
What exactly is it that is entering our flesh?

From one moment to the next rage breaks out
And destroys everything in its path.
It's as if our god were not giving us time
To adapt to these shifts in common reality.

Let me look into my inner sanctum, there where
The face of another matters to me or not,
Where the illusion of happiness persuades me
To lower my guard, to neglect preparation.

This world is changing towards new world
While our soul insists on old worship,
The earth is being forced out of the picture
By earth as habitat for merciful human beings.

I would like to be the sort of person who
Casts no aspersion and forgives every slight,
So it stands to reason that to that end I must be
Given opportunities for revenge and blame.

I lower my head and hope that the light will
Enter my heart. I continue with my work
So that others will have the benefit of my gains.
I search in my past for the fruits of wisdom.

You who look out to stars in space and imagine
An end or a beginning of the universe will soon
Be scolded by your human spirit within you.
Incarnate spirit seeks brothers and sisters for life.

* * *

Faith and Suffering

1

In the end we decided we really
Had no choice, so we joined the crowds
That had gathered near the cathedral.
Some had brought their belongings
On handcarts or they had bolted
Bicycles together to help them
Transport their babes across the river.

We all felt we had a right to complain
To the authorities who had misled us.
Now, of course, no one was in sight
Who might assume responsibility.
The campfires were quickly extinguished
And the horses fed one last time
Before we moved on to the mountains.

Among us were beggars in unprincipled
Collusion with politicians and shabby
Members of the defunct aristocracy
Weaved in and out of the serried ranks.
They offered drinks of water and
Words of advice where spirits were low.
For a time the delusion of purpose reigned.

In the foothills we buried our dead.
A young Chinese woman had given
Birth to twins. We were shocked by how
Her husband treated her, as if he
Cared nothing for her. The nights
Were colder now. Snow gleamed
On the massive peaks in the distance.

*

2

Will you not please explain to me
Why I am still in such pain? Surely
I have satisfied the elemental spirits by now.
I have been at it since this morning,
When you informed me you no longer
Wished to travel on the same road with me.

This is surely wicked how much we depend
On old habits and comforts, as if humanity
Had to be earned, perhaps by sacrifice of
One's dearest wishes and ambitions.
Now I feel that my mind is benighted and
My contact with human beings is severed.

I suppose by now I should be able to yield
Gracefully to pain and fear due to change,
Change which I had neither desired nor
Charted. I am nearly out of my wits
After these several days of grim frustration
When nothing I touched flourished.

They will say he has no morality, he
Flings his ancestor's ashes to the wind.
I am getting cranky in my old age,
Tied with chains to my principles
And afraid to act out what really bothers me.
You, you alone could set me straight.

They have departed for the mountains and
Left me behind on my three-legged stool,
A fool's cap on my head, in my hand a rattle.
At night badgers dig up grubs near my fire.
Look, this used to be a perfectly groomed lawn
Now it looks like a potato field in winter.

*

3

Oh, I can hear the music in the distance,
Not fife and drum but oboe and clarinet in
Sweet unison. Nonetheless my brain hums
And the wheezing of my lungs alarms me.

Shall I describe my penthouse at the top of
This monumental skyscraper? The view
Across miles of winding river bed, beach huts
In flames again after a late night party.

I have not swum in this pool for weeks.
The walls are mostly windows which have
Not been cleaned since the earthquake and
Now no one dares risk his life with repairs.

Happily I have enough tinned food to last me
A year or more, so I have no worries, merely
The boredom of being alone in the world.
There are several of us in this forsaken city.

You may take it that we know of one another
And while external contact, by sight or
Telephone, is no longer possible, we will
Learn to commune from within our spirit.

The human spirit, after all, is common to all,
Only sometimes it takes a time of oppression
To alert us to what has been possible for years.
It is a power I will eventually be able to wield.

Today, with the help of my field glasses, I can
Make someone out in the field near that
Collapsed building. He wears a fool's cap and
Repeatedly returns to his three-legged stool.

*

4

I will not be forced out of my routine.
Some are born to work and I shall
Continue to work no matter what happens.
Psychic conditions would, as usual,
Draw all attention to themselves if we
Did not insist on keeping our wits about us.

If I had not, long ago, decided to draw a
Circle around me, an invisible zone which
Defines for me how far I am willing to be
Influenced by matters beyond my control,
I would now stand helpless before this
Onslaught of unidentifiable mischance.

Most of the time the quick cure is available,
Handy enough for anyone with a few bob,
But that only makes sense if survival is
One's prerogative, and not those precious
Works which are willing to arrive at our
Doorstep if we hold out under pressure.

Also one jealously accumulates new skills.
These freakish illnesses nowadays point
To exceptional spirit data which we resist,
Hence our ill-being. A degree of repentance
Is advisable while we tackle the results of
Our ignorant reactions, our inattentiveness.

My brain at this moment is convulsed.
Behind my eyes shock after shock squanders
Energy I might have employed in order to
Free what I mean when I refer to myself.
My hands shake. Someone in that penthouse
Spotted me after all and waived to me.

*

5

It's a risky business, this
Living from day to day as if
One had no control over one's life.
If people cannot decided how their
Future will reflect their aspirations
They are bound to become downcast
Or furious, and we must prevent that.
So we surround them with planned events.
In fact we turn them into planned things,
To allow them to believe that at least
Someone knows what is going on and will
Make unfailing decisions in the direction of
More unfailing decisions. Lord knows,
We are only doing our best, they say,
And good gracious, they may be right.

We are always looking for volunteers
Who will lay their life on the line for
The rest of us who have not much life left.
That sounds defeatist, I know. If we could
Predict who is going to die from being sick
And who is going to recuperate and end up
Stronger than ever before, why, then we could
Terrify the population into playing their cards
Close to their chest until election time, or
At least until God's anointed make their move.
I suggest we keep our ear close to the ground.
Repent and seek the kingdom of heaven, yes,
Let's face it, that sums it up, and why we pay
Taxes after that puzzles me no end.
It's democracy or unconditional love.

*

6

Faith know the enemy and forgives him.
Wisdom thrives in the presence of the enemy.
This is what I spoke to the mountain
And the mountain removed itself.

A joyful person spoke of his experiences
And even though he related many misadventures
The animals approached and listened.
When he spoke to them they turned away.

It is well to believe what one hears,
Then the bad will remove itself from the good.
Justice is a friend of the simple minded.
They do not seek it, so it comes to them.

Death both kills and gives birth.
At once it hides and reveals.
We would never know which way to turn
If death did not stand at the crossroads.

There are lies which are well told to music
But poorly told in the desert or in a wood.
We will never persuade a man of the truth
By forbidding him to lie.

The tragedy of the outside or the inside.
The mystery of the outward and the inward.
In order to pass through the eye of the needle
We allow the tragedy to affect us.

Two-thousand years of history
Enlivened by a few rays of light.
Meanwhile a tiger prowls at the perimeter
And a gnat prompts us to action.

*

7

There were those who made life uncomfortable
For the children in our midst. There had been
Much dispute about the need for an upbringing
When a boy cursed his teacher and was
Promptly chastised by him. This struck
The rest of us as most unfortunate.

When I accidentally broke one of my friend's
Precious wineglasses he quickly broke the other.
Those who observed this misunderstood it.
We agreed there was no way of explaining
Without destroying the virtue of this deed.

Is the time ever appropriate for drastic measures?
Can it ever fail to surround a sin with silence?
We marched at the head of a column
Until we arrived at the seashore, whereupon
Some wept, while others fell about laughing.

Good and bad will never fit into a single container.
Either the good will spill over or the bad leak out.
Therefore the government based on an idea
Causes a refugee problem for that country's
Neighbours which realize now how they were at fault
When they behaved like that in the past.

I cannot make myself fall asleep. But I can
Make myself wake up. The same goes for the
Understanding. Reason will not be bullied
But accepts invitations. It is a great mystery
That we take so long to accept a stranger.

There comes a time when we are no longer
Prompted to distinguish between the upper
And the lower. Now we simply reach into god's
Larder and dispense victual. The cause facilitates
The effect and virtue is automatic.

*

8

Between faith in justice and injustice suffered
Nothing can go wrong. Always we remove
Ourselves from the picture to destroy it.
The picture blocks out the image and then
The image can no longer be symbolic.
It takes only one missile with a single warhead
To destroy the entire population of a city.

The fact that the modern world has been
Tragically flawed for two-thousand years
Should not surprise us when we look at
The foundation upon which it is erected.
The chaos of the ancient world was divided
Into two opposing halves, neither of which
Could make cosmic sense without the other.

What is it that stands at the fountainhead
And offers wholeness to him who buries
His self in the earth and waits for it to sprout?
What we call god is no magical formula
But simply our greater self seeking to join us.
This much I can say without arrogance.
To proceed I confess the mystery that is god.

This again activates my wish to be truly
Human. All the earth and its wonders are now
Involved in every moment of my existence.
I apologize for being so ignorant in the past.
I seek a mate and we raise several children.
The god I once knew reintroduces himself.
What I know now I cannot entirely reveal.

*

9

A wind blows. A seagull longs
For the open ocean. I too, this morning,
Am bereft of freedom but shall avoid
Speaking the nonsense of the sage.

All is not well that ends its days
Looking for love in diverse ways
And never finding for not doing,
Never loving, only wooing.

Therefore never end your days,
You have but one day to see to,
To see to and to break or mend,
While all your days you suspend.

A virtuous father loved his daughter
Until she took up with a bad man.
Who told him that was a bad man?
Let him continue to love his daughter.

That cantankerous old fox
Has cheated me of a thousand pounds.
Has he not rather cheated himself
Of mending his cantankerous ways?

The brightness of her blue eyes,
Oh how they promise a heaven!
Perhaps for you, my good man.
The two of you should get together.

Narrowly defeated they lay like
Beached whales on the river bank,
Little realizing the inappropriateness
Of who, where and why they were.

*

10

Let me indulge, just for a little while,
This delusion that the weather and my moods
Are separate entities, to be juggled,
To be connected by a great causeway,
Absurdly great, self-made, ever so comic.

Why do you not stop me? Let me think.
You too like a little self-indulgence.
Let us hope that we never meet while we
String the beads of hope on a cat's whisker.

*

11

I chance to close my eyes and a
Cartload of manure lands on my lawn.
Does it matter at all that I was not
Ready for this universal donation?

Like a madman I begin to dig,
I nearly destroy my lawn in the effort
To justify the cause of universal selection.
A mistake! The manure was not for me.

Heavy eyes cannot help themselves.
Leaden portals foreclose the day.
Something is in the air which reminds me
Of my duty to my fellow man.

*

12

The perfect man dispenses perfection.
Oh look, there, a perfect man. He is
Dispensing perfection. Let us avoid him.
We prefer to squat behind the scullery,
Surviving on scraps from the kitchen,
On the odd curse from the cook.

*

13

The testimony of fear and pain is fact, he shouted
and threw himself into the maelstrom.
We little children dance and sing
And play our games of silent wondering.

*

14

Suddenly a massive weakness unnerved me
And I had to be rushed off the stage before I
Embarrassed the rest of the cast who had
Cast-iron stomachs and hearts of pure gold.

*

15

Pain and fear appear not to exist but so that
You might exist, you and I, perhaps eating from
The same plate, drinking from the same jug.

*

16

I am thoroughly fatigued, I breathe heavily
Through nose and mouth, my chest heaves.
Has there been an earthquake in Taiwan?
Perhaps I am merely being a little foolish.

*

17

A dreadful apparition on the horizon
Reminds me of myself as afraid and in pain.
Now I have been invited to declare myself
To the neighbour's wife who has a sick cat.

How am I to console myself over the fact
That nothing is as bad as it seems?
Am I not the tragedy queen of the neighbourhood?
And now this terrific fatigue!

*

18

If we do not accept that two-thousand years ago
The human race began to evolve, which means
That those best fitted for the new condition
Would survive while the others would fade away,

And if we cannot come to terms with the fact
That human natural faith alone is required
If we are to do the work that will establish us
As new beings in the light of day, then in truth

We may share the fate of the dodo.
We will certainly be remembered for a while
As those who insisted on carrying on the
Popular tradition but we will then be forgotten.

*

19

Ladies and gentlemen, in here we inherit!
If only I could persuade you to take seriously
What goes on in here, when we are not looking,
While in ourselves we still see cause for reform.

*

20

It is good that the glaciers melt.
What is a little extra warmth,
A little extra water?
This is still a mild consequence of
Good spirit rejected.

It is no great shakes
That the oceans are sullied
And the forests ravaged.
The cause of this troubles me more:
No true community.

If men were to cherish women
And women to cherish men,
How soon would the species flourish
And the populations settle down.
But beauty is falsified.

Surely heaven is willing
To guide us in our projects,
Each individually, self-effacing,
Recognizing human nature as
An unspoiled world.

*

21

How can we possibly insist
That the up and the down must be divorced,
That the left and right shall be separated,
That the rich and the poor can be distinguished.

Can the stream flow in a straight line?
Can the same breath enter and leave?
How will we bring ourselves to love
If we prefer the high to the low?

* * *

22

Believe this with your whole heart:
Human nature is gentle.

* * *

Holiday in Italy

Tuscany, Umbria

1

Within the cool spaces of
Overhanging boughs of
Oaks, their patient branches
Suffering for us the monstrous heat,

We compile a few thoughts,
A few images to keep order.
In the mottled shade on the
Ground a few grasses sprout.

Breeze upon breeze, then
An orange-tip, a catkin
suspended by spider-thread,
a fly buzzing, again, buzzing.

Dry leaves, gravel crunching underfoot,
Another green lizard rustling,
Flies dancing, no human beings
Dare wake in this heat.

*

2

Seated on the wall beside the gate
I think of the time when I shall recall
Precisely this moment, when pen in hand
I allow one drop of history to accumulate.

When someone takes the trouble to carve
Survival-space out of the wilderness
One cannot help wondering how long before
The stones are once again disassembled.

A tree's life is like a pleasant dream
And a wood like the legends of a people,
The earth expressing its desire for light
Prior to humanity, however in expectation –

Truly this heat tends to be burdensome
All over Tuscany and perhaps beyond
Where the juice in Umbrian grapes is sweetening
While melons ripen, anticipating our gratitude.

*

3

The human brain is an unusual organ
And mostly unfamiliar to those who drink sleep.
Its receptivity to pure images is phenomenal
And lo, its capacity for knowledge is endless.

A new breed of humans has lately
Come into existence and for them their brain's
Activity is as natural as the plough to the farmer
And they carry in their flesh the future seed.

Prioritize all this fabulous experience
In spite of the collective ignorance + anger,
In the knowledge that for you not a stone is turned
But new property flashes in heaven.

I believe that the sound made by the truth
As it seeps into existence over the horizon
Continues to reverberate through succeeding generations
If recorded in genuine respect for the gods.

*

4

Years ago my legs were
Less sluggish in the morning
And this walk uphill would have
Cost me no effort at all but
The stream of appreciation runs deeper now,
What with life enhanced by mortality.

In the distance the hills cause
Vision to question itself.
At seven in the morning in Tuscany
Not far from the piled streets of Siena
Dew still stains the shoe-leather
And the cocks are still crowing.
A slice of moon hangs above the oaks.

This cracked, sun-parched,
Spider-webbed playground for
Lizards and at night the glow worms,
Roaming bats, then swifts en masse
Darting in and out of that tower –
Lord knows, when I try to be popular
They simply ignore me.

*

5

The woods awaken,
Tree trunks flash sunlight;
I practically disappear
To let the secret voices speak.

Every imaginable patch of earth
Possesses its own local demon.
A squirrel travels through the canopy
In leaps and bounds, carefree.

Familiar spirits commonly brood
Slightly beneath the surface
Where the perceptive soul registers
The dreams activating the world.

Birdsong here, automobile traffic
There behind thoughtless perimeters;
Cold stone outcropping, pleasant –
Deer and boar concealed now.

Men can be a bit of a curse
Throughout the year, on the landscape
But somehow long gaps in history
Accentuate the unknown. Catastrophes correct.

*

6

Near Siena
In the cool shade of a stone hut,
Gnarled olive, unripe fig,
Butterflies levitating over fleabane,
A pheasant's harsh note of alarm,
Layer upon layer of spider web over
Parched soil, cracked, rotovated, cracked,
Midges, cicadas, beetles, flies,
A shotgun shell case, long spent.
Sporadic croaking of frogs,
Rusting farm machinery piled
Under huddled cypresses.

Something in me chooses to notice this,
To draw attention to itself for your sake.

It may be learned how to be grateful
For a cooling breeze at midday.

The grassy verge speckled by meadow bindweed;
Firewood, carefully stacked, wild oat,
Foxtails, ragwort, hawkweed,
A field full of rye.

*

7

It was exhausting work
Dragging himself up into the hills,
Away from those who said they knew better.
The night coolness was withdrawing into the woods.

Wherever he looked were things that died
In order to live again – a peculiar arrangement.
Beetles settled on asphodel blooms.
He imagined the sky lay in tatters.

Suddenly a cloud of midges rose
And dispersed into the azure.
He knew he would not live long,
Not in this present form in any case.

*

8

So many butterflies illuminated the earth
That the longest moment could not contain them.
Hunters shot the song birds,
Drove wedges between earth and man.

He regulated his heartbeat to fit in with
The largesse of the countryside.
Daily trauma prevented the population
From eating and drinking at the messianic table.

It was, finally, as if a distant barking dog
Could alter the pattern of the universe.
The ideals of the age stood about laughing
Because nothing would suit these incontinent people.

*

9

For me personally the great church in Siena
Gave cause for complaint.
I did not wish it so
But all that art everywhere did not fool me.
What had they left in their hearts
Except a myriad motivations for sophisticated cruelty
Once they downed hammer, chisel and brush?
However very likely no one noticed.

*

10

He enlarged the power of the word
Until it encompassed the contemporary spirit.
The pictures fled in consternation
And images assembled around god's throne.

He laboured until leisure reigned
Supreme over the world's finite gestures.
His own position was clear from the start:
That one among an infinite number.

Look at the trees today and tell me
Can anything be more beautiful?
Reach for our harp. No enchantment, please!
Help me come down to earth within myself.

*

11

When age overtook him
He fought bitterly.
Why should the strength of the flesh
Not cede priority to the good spirit's
Gentle embodiment?

He chose his final task with care.
His youth had undergone a renewal.
Boyhood had largely been wasted
But the muse had awoken in the young man.
Then maturity hoisted its twofold flag.

*

12

Clearly at any moment pain might
Draw the curtain on cheerful awareness.
Then fear exaggerates, anger intensifies
This challenge to crippling mind-set.

He eased himself into the day's deformities,
Brandished no weapon to repulse demons,
Only relied on that inward safety feature
That comfort zone installed in year zero.

When the white sheet came down he paused
And acknowledged the power of divine personality.
Pinprick incidents revealed profound meaning,
Involution suggested by a clear sky.

When work became the coiled spring in him
He gloried in his manhood, and why not?
Because greater glory awaited the meek one,
Mindful of the realm's cultivation.

*

13

Can anyone avoid the next painful crisis?
One inadvertently buys into the work ethic
Until the next swallow unzips the field of vision
To belie all terminal strategies.

Or do we misinterpret how all beings
Delight in the union of zest and survival?
The eagle soars and soaring finds
His eye attracted by the insouciant hare.

Let be what would be. There's pleasant limitation
To individual capacity. Our thought runs
To adoration, bewilderment, mockery and then
Returns to haunt the inturned self again.

*

14

Judicious use of strong language
Separates those who cherish an affiliation
With truth, beauty and good food
From those who no longer give a shit.

No, please, don't misunderstand me now.
My tastes are as simple as those of a
Five-year-old hankering after ice cream.
I like Signorelli's depiction of the pit.

Besides, why should a display of beastliness
Anger the gods more than the heinous
Liberties taken by those who speak
The polite language, the political lingo?

The scientific gibberish, the proprieties of the prelates –
They spring to mind when I clear my plate
Of all scraps after a messianic meal.
One truly conceived image brings joy.

*

15

As soon as he heard of the invasion
He stopped all intercourse with the mutants
And withdrew to his chalet in the mountains
Where security and comfort awaited him.

Naturally there were many primitive associations
Which brought his digestion to a halt.
His private inclinations no longer counted,
Or shall we say: He fled from himself too.

When news came that the insurgents had been
In part repulsed, in part assimilated,
He ventured out into society incognito,
Eager to take up his work once more.

The children were the first to accept his message
Which consisted of a revision of ancient values
Shot through with the spirit of high noon,
When shade fails, to reappear elsewhere.

*

16

My first meeting with the Queen of Sparta
Came off rather well, I believe,
For she had cast off all pretensions to being
A mythical creature, shrouded in ambiguity,
While I, as usual, laid my cards on the table.

Polite conversation, conventional observances
Had duly given way to confessional exchange,
The times being such that policy no longer
Held sway over personal revelation.

It was the time of the Athenian arrogance at its height
When the Persian threat could not yet serve
To excuse that criminal self-indulgence
Which later gave birth to a splendid culture.

As evening drew in over wine and sweetmeats,
We speculated that the narrow Spartan mentality
Would eventually succumb to an inward richness,
However not until after much suffering.

*

17

The lake lay at his feet,
A vast expanse of solicitude,
A bright response to perfect blue sky.

From his fortified promontory he oversaw
The settlement of the shores over the years
and he rejoiced at the prospect of companionship.

Alas, the gods had decreed
That a great subterranean upheaval
Should cast all present knowledge into confusion.

He had catalogued and annotated,
Had attempted to make himself indispensible
To material progress and success.

Too late it dawned on him
That the lake's symbolic significance
Was no match for its concrete liveliness.

They buried him, along with his possessions,
His accumulated wealth and weaponry
And then turned, to worship in realty.

*

18

Contempt for people invariably involves
A degree of dependence on popularity.

Neither, of course, does total freedom
Prerequire a fondness of people.

'The people' are a myth, brain-fodder
For manipulators of the world's appearances.

We speak of the earth's population, however
When will the earth be truly inhabited?

The first human being allowed himself to be
Killed for his unpopular representations.

*

19

His manner and intent were nice;
Day in day out he strove and aped.
*‚Der Mensch der sich zu helfen weiß
Entspricht dem Gott der hilflos lebt.'*[i]

* * *

[i] The man who knows how to help himself
Corresponds to the god who lives without help.

Index of First Lines

* * *
* *

Index of First Lines in alphabetic order

* * *

* *

*

www.ingramcontent.com/pod-product-compliance
Ingram Content Group UK Ltd.
Pitfield, Milton Keynes, MK11 3LW, UK
UKHW020418250726
13967UKWH00007B/2708

9 781794 874343